Cat

Written by Ruth Young
Illustrated by Bob Ostrom

Hooked On Phonics®

ISBN 1-887942-46-7

Do you see my nice new hat?

"What is that?"
"Is that your cat?"

My cat looks just
like any cat—

but he turns into
this and that!

He's where I keep
my nice new bat.
He's where I hide
my nice white rat.

He's where I store
my big red hat.
He keeps my artwork
nice and flat.

When it rains, I don’t get wet.
My cat is there, and I’m all set.

When I am hot,
he is a pool.

My pals and I
stay nice and cool.

And if we want to see a show,
my cat is where we like to go.

Sometimes my cat
becomes a box.
He's big and green
with shiny locks.

When I lost my teddy bear,
I checked my box, and he was there.

When I come home
and want to chat,
I like to go
and see my cat.

I never know what I will see,
a dog, a pig, a goat, or bee.

When we need a nice big boat,
my cat is there, and off we float.

When we play handball
on the wall,

my cat is there.
He is the ball!

When it gets dark, he needs to eat.
That's when my cat gets very sweet.

He comes home for
a fishy treat,
and cleans his dish
up nice and neat.

My cat and I are sleepy now.
My cat and I will take a bow.
Good-bye.
Good-bye.
Meow!
Meow!